# To Bury or Burn

Selected Poems

by

Judith Robbins

Copyright © 2019 by Judith Robbins

All rights reserved. No part of this book may be reproduced or transmitted in any form or by any means without written permission of the author.

ISBN 978-1-943424-53-5
Library of Congress Control Number: 2019951038

Cover photo of The Writing House by Rachel Robbins

Photograph of My Son in Brooklyn, 1995, by Chris Selicious

North Country Press
Unity, Maine

## ACKNOWLEDGMENTS

*Church World*       Suspension

*Paterson Literary Review*     The Dance

*Rockland Courier Gazette*     Getting to the Source

*Sisters Today*     You Can Get There from Here

I acknowledge with gratitude Jack Faling, Claire Hersom, Pat Chaney, and Gay Grant for their critical readings and reviews of the manuscript; Patricia Newell, editor and publisher of North Country Press; and my family—Jon, Hannah, Patrick, Rachel and Joshua—for their support and encouragement.

Other books by Judith Robbins
　　*The North End* (North Country Press, 2016)
　　*The Bookbinder's Wife* (North Country Press, 2018)

For Hannah, Patrick, Rachel and Joshua

# Table of Contents

Today / 1
Commit. Commit.———. / 2
Clean Your Room / 3
Smelling Salts / 4
*Carpe diem* / 5
Memorializing Heaney Memorializing / 6
Letter to Grace Paley, Re "In the Bus" / 7
After a Morning with English Poets / 8
Note to Self / 9
Marginalia / 10
"She continued writing all her life . . ." / 11
The Reach of Cliché / 12
Better than Bacitracin / 13
Getting to the Source / 14
Ready, Set, ——! / 15
Ready to Write? / 16
To Seek the Un-balance / 17
Exhortation Upon Sitting Down to Write / 18
Something like a Sonnet / 19
Pen in Hand / 20
Platform for Healing / 21
The Dance / 22
The Man Behind the Fish Counter / 23
The Neighbors Are on Vacation / 24
Suspension / 25
It's Monday, Wash Day at Our House / 26
All I Want for Christmas / 27
Following the Full Hip Replacement / 28
Ode to Egg Salad Sandwiches / 29

Poems from The Mikie Cycle / 30
Resurrection / 34
Is This Adoption Legal? / 35
Photograph of My Son in Brooklyn, 1995 / 36
September 11, 2018 / 38
Homing Pigeon / 39
A Question / 40
Left with questions about / 41
Night Visitors / 42
After the Blizzard / 43
March, You've Arrived / 44
The Battle for Spring / 45
Gotcha / 46
March 12 / 47
Thoughts during a Snow Squall / 48
ShhShhhShhhh! / 49
Presque Isle, Maine: Snow, 5/16/16 / 50
I Ask and Receive / 51
Birds in Wind / 52
Tribulation / 53
Dalliance / 54
O Holy Day! / 55
Notice for Penobscot Bay, Maine / 56
Thoughts in Late September / 57
A Child's Prayer / 58
I Skirt the Violets / 59
May I Have This Dance? / 60
Yes, Virginia, There Is a God / 61
Deep into April / 62
Housekeeping / 63
Lost in Limbo / 64
A Dream After My Mother's Death / 65
You Can Get There from Here / 67

To Eat or Be Eaten / 68
Tightrope Walking / 69
Parallels / 71
In the Woods / 73
For a Friend: R.I.P. / 74
Father's Day / 75
And Then? / 76
Hello, Goodbye / 77
To Bury or Burn / 78

# Today

It is early; it is light; it is a new day.
Be in it with full consciousness and joy.
The world and life await you.
Arrive fully dressed and ready to work,
to do, to make, to be part of the fabric
of this day, this new day in the world.

**Commit. Commit. ———.**

*... the moment one definitely commits*
*oneself, then Providence moves too.*
                    W.H. Murray
            The Scottish Himalayan Expedition


To walk from periphery to center is the longest walk
one makes in a given life. No matter when
it happens—at 7, 15, or 73—no matter, only
that it happens, lands you at the creating center
committed to fulfill the work of your life,
most immediately, the work of the day.

Who's to say but you what the work is
discerned in silence and fed by a hundred moments
of deep joy. Go ahead. Take the walk of commitment
from periphery to center. I double-dare you
to fall down and kiss the ground that is creation
of which you are a part, so help you God.

## Clean Your Room

The broom of self-discipline is behind the door
where you left it when you began before
to introduce order into your life again.

**Smelling Salts**

Everyone is being called
out into their lives, those lives lying
about like Victorian women
suffering from neurasthenia

and learning through their suffering
that they are the shapers of those lives
for better, for worse, for richer, for poorer.
All parts of the self wedded, they take the field.

## *Carpe diem*

I don't want to miss the boat.
That possibility troubles my dreams
as it did last night when I saw the boat

still at the dock, engines thrumming,
chuffing, purring. Would I come aboard
this time? I turned back into the day

and worked my way up the street
to wakefulness, and whatever
that held for me.

## Memorializing Heaney Memorializing

As poet-survivor among your peers
the task of memorializing fell to you

again and again—in memory of Richard,
of Tom, of John Hewitt—in *Seeing Things*;
they rose again to life under your pen

in poems filled with your humanity
still intact. While you outlived many

it was finally you for whom death came
thirsty, a-search, and drinking you quickly
lest the glass spill and anything of you be lost.

## Letter to Grace Paley, Re "In the Bus"

I gave away the monograph you autographed for me,
handing it to me as casually as the morning paper.
I treasured that poem and hung it beside
the Regulator clock on our kitchen wall
whose pendulum was a message of time passing

like the content of your poem, which exhorted you
and so the reader, to begin again. Decades have passed
since then, and only the clock remains, the monograph
gone to a young writer, who attributed her writing life
to your inspiration. She had sought your signature

in Provincetown, where you were conducting a writing workshop. That autograph drowned with much else
in a flooding storm, she needed the monograph more
than I who had long ago internalized the poem's message: To
begin again, and so I did and do.

# After a Morning with English Poets

My head is full of poetry not my own.
With Tennyson's Sir Bedivere I mourn
for Arthur, going forth in his black barge,
his bloodied head resting in the lap of a queen,
barely alive but admonishing us
to pray for his immortal soul.

Herrick admonishes in other words,
to gather rosebuds while we may
for tomorrow those very same flowers
will die, as one day so will you and I.

But then to Donne, stripped bare of career
for love of a girl. He speaks hope to her
      and so to us:

*If our two loves be one, or thou and I*
*Love so alike that none do slacken, none can die.*

# Note to Self

*All goes onward and outward, nothing collapses,*
*And to die is different from what anyone supposed,*
*and luckier.*
                    Walt Whitman, "Song of Myself"

Walt Whitman celebrated himself. Without blame
apology or braggadocio, he claimed his plot
of ground and planted his flag, as men on the moon

did a hundred years hence. A prophet, yes,
and nature's priest, but also a man
relishing the role he knew was his as poet

and nurse, as it turned out, to Civil War wounded.
Like Frederick Douglass of that same era, who wrote
his slave narrative—adding to it, subtracting from it

as the years heaped up behind him—so did Whitman
himself add and subtract. They practiced a mathematics of
poetry and justice. Self-pity had no place in the lives

of these men, who knew the decades allotted to them
were a rosary of sorts, each bead a poem, or an action
that spelt the future.

# Marginalia

I open to Rilke's "Blue Hydrangeas"
and see written "July 1976"

in the margin. I marvel anew
at his blue letter paper washed out
like a child's apron no longer used.

I marvel too at the 25 years
that have brought me to this place,
how in 25 more I'll be an old woman.

MacIntyre translates: "One feels
how short the little life has been."

Indeed, but then the blue renews
itself in one last cluster.

# "She continued writing all her life ...

persevering through war, exile, imprisonment
and the loss of her fortune." So writes
the translator Wendy Chen of Li Qingzhao
known for her *ci*—her poems set to music.

The gauntlet thrown down, I pick it up,
not having had to persevere through war,
exile, imprisonment or loss of fortune,
my cup of history and responsibilities

shouldered over many years is what
I have to offer, not that of the Chinese poet,
her life complicated by much beyond her control

but children, they are what fills the cup
with laundry, cooking, transportation
doctoring, comforting, encouraging
daily emergence into their lives.

Notwithstanding differences—a woman's
life is a woman's life—I accept the challenge
of her life, and continue writing mine.

## The Reach of Cliché

*A good cry.* Having one
presupposes feeling
better after
than you did before.
What about
*a bad cry?* Is there such
a thing? I imagine
the cause: a broken heart
unmendable, whether
through death, or worse, betrayal,
wanting to have a good cry,
but not knowing how to begin.

## Better than Bacitracin

Write into the wound with the ink that heals,
the black blood that marks the place
where poison entered in.
Write into the wound with the ink that heals.

## Getting to the Source

I dug the well an inch at a time
through matted grass, soil and gravel
clay and soft rock, down and down
'til at nine feet the water flowed.

The vein was slow when it first bled
but now the channel cleared of dross
pumps pure from the heart of earth
and cannot be turned off.

## Ready, Set, —!

Be gentle. Be slow
until the moment comes
when all is fast, and so will you be
fast, fasted as you are from all detritus
that had clung like barnacles to your psyche
and held you apart from all you would do
and be. Now is the hour to act. Scraped
clean you are able beyond your knowing
to fulfill in the simplest and most satisfying
ways the call on the rest of your life.

**Ready to Write?**


On the slant top of the schoolmaster desk
rest your cheek on the white paper.
Close to the wood, listen for the song

of the ax, for the drop of the blade,
for the lightning that rives the apple
tree with promise of spring and new

growth. The pain of riving done,
become yourself.

## To Seek the Un-balance

You have tasted poetry with a silver spoon
but have never been consumed yourself
by the need and will to write first and then
to attend the rest—cleaning, harvesting,
volunteering—seeking the infamous balance.

No. Seek the un-balance. Allow the scale's
weight to drop heavy on the side of writing
not making allowance for all else
but saving pride of place for poetry
ever first in the Muse's intent for you.

## Exhortation Upon Sitting Down to Write

Go with your first instinct.
Get it down quick before your critic
cuts in to take over the lead
for the dance of this poem
that's only begun.
Go with the one who brought you.

## Something like a Sonnet

Fly-specked and dusty and perfectly mine
this space for poetry out of time
where worry troubles not the moted air.
Once over the threshold nary a care
can raise its fleecy bothersome head
demanding attention I've already shed
when doffing my coat and winter hat
and lighting a fire. Done,
I assume the writer's seat
pick up the pen and relish the heat.
*Ink on paper, word on tongue ...*
a chant that can be daily sung
to invoke the Muse in all its glory
and contribute one note to the human story.

## Pen in Hand

I grope in the darkness
seeking the lineaments of your face.

My fingers made for handling matter
your divinity passes through untouched

except for my longing, which
registers, I trust, with you.

## Platform for Healing

A friend diagnosed with cancer
describes the reality of how it feels
to be beaten up over and over again
with pain, nausea from treatment
to treatment, then body-slammed
onto the floor, with cancer calling
out the challenge: *Now show me
what you've got.* It is in that moment,
she says, the gauntlet thrown down
and the body a mess of disease
that the choice is made to stagger
up to a standing position, and with
tears of anger and determination,
new life begins to build. First
floor, second floor, up to the third,
where treatment ends and hair
grows back, not straight this time
but curly.

# The Dance

The thought of Zelda Fitzgerald
dancing herself to death-by-fire
on the top floor of an insane asylum

gives me pause in the presence
of fire always, with fear attending.
Once scorched, any one of us thinks

twice about where the extinguisher is;
then memorizes, "In case of fire ..."
before putting on dancing shoes.

## The Man Behind the Fish Counter

I was somebody wanting to buy some fish
needing a little help, a little advice, inexperienced
as I am in matters of fish. And you?
The man behind the fish counter? Tall, dark and
burly, maybe too burly for the handling
of naked fish, skun, filleted as they were,
without their scaly armor, heads and tails
lopped off; you more of a butcher than
I'd have thought. Your snarl when you spoke
made me wonder whom you were seeing
when you looked at me, an old lady
in tennis shoes. Was it mother? sister?
grandmother? wife? Who drove the anger
as you drove the knife into fish?

# The Neighbors Are on Vacation

No clank of iron on iron.
No bang of a dump truck's dropped tailgate.
No tumble of four-foot lengths of wood to the ground.

No chorus of skidder or snowplow engines
severally humming or grinding alive
in the pre-dawn cold of late December—
All of this gone to Florida with the neighbors.

Blessed silence drifts down, and grateful we walk
the snowy ground, relieved of the constant sound
of what it means to make a living in Maine.

## Suspension

My world is filled with hanging things—
pots, pans and cutting boards
sifters, spoons, and time-dried apples—
Things. And people too are hanging,
ancestral photos on the walls.
Surfaces. Flat faces. No depth, but then
move on to the eyes and there reflections are
of pots, pans, cutting boards, time-
dried apples pungent with hidden life.

## It's Monday, Wash Day at Our House

While clothes are drying on the line
I write a line and then another about
hiding underwear behind the sheets
on the front line. Victorian secrets are
kept in original ways, washed and dried,
folded and stored in the linen closet
upstairs. When they're hung on the line
for all to see, they're called "dirty laundry,"
and so you may understand why
the underwear is masked by clean sheets.
It's Monday, wash day at our house.

## All I Want for Christmas ...

For Christmas I want an Irish breakfast
of smoked salmon and scrambled eggs
and freshly baked soda bread that satisfies
something deeper than simply taste,
a broiled tomato halved—Don't forget that.

No vapid boiled cabbage, with milk and
potatoes and meat for high tea. No, it's
the breakfast, the Irish breakfast with Yeats'
"Lake Isle of Innisfree" printed on napkins ample
for spills or for blotting sentimental tears

as someone reads, "I will arise and go now,
and go to Innisfree," while I dip a buttered
crust in the hot black tea.

## Following the Full Hip Replacement

An alien is spending the night with me.
It wants us to sleep in the same bed.
How can I say no to this guest,
hospitality being a rule of the house.
I wring my hands in consternation.
Why did I ever sign on for this?
Too late to change my mind.
This alien is here for all of the nights
of the rest of my life. Nothing to do
but soldier on, remembering the pain
before it moved in with me.

## Ode to Egg Salad Sandwiches

Enamored of all about the beloved
—by the eye, the hand, the trembling mouth—
the lover is undone.
For me, it's egg salad sandwiches.

Inspired by a distant view of The People
—breeding, borning, living, dying—
the revolutionary is undone.
But for me, it's egg salad sandwiches.

Give me a wedding where the budget is low
guests on folding chairs row on row
plates piled high with the hens' sweet roe.
Yes, for me it's egg salad sandwiches.

Soggy white triangles with hardening crust
preferably no lettuce but mayo a must.
The newlyweds plight their troth and their trust.
As for me, it's egg salad sandwiches.

**Poems from The Mikie Cycle**
written following the death-by-coyote of our tabby cat

*My light blown early
out, I sit in the dark.*

8/15/05

When does grief become unseemly?
Too many days have you mourned this cat, I hear
in my inner critic's ear, but I cannot dam the river.
How many days are too many?
How long did David mourn his son
crying, Absalom! Absalom!
If only I had died instead of you.

8/26/05

Imagine looking into the eyes
of bobcat, coyote, mountain lion
where any reflection of you is an accident of light.

You have no meaning beyond being creature—
predator or prey remains to be seen—
images of lion and lamb together scattered by confrontation.

Fables dissolve in mutual assessment,
in cold curiosity, the greater fear,
the longer claw, determining who will prevail.

8/29/05

Nearly three weeks have exhausted themselves

in tears since your body was torn. My heart
torn too, if truth be told. Hurricane winds blow
fresh today; the wound remains

open. Rains in the Gulf and Lake Ponchetrain
surge over levees at New Orleans. A wall
of water floats the caskets of the dead
who have lain in state atop the ground.

Those floating dead and huddled living
swirl in the eye of a storm of common grief.
I claim that grief for you, my cat
torn by coyote from life, like a babe

from its mother's arms in the flooding streets.
I claim that grief for all who weep and suffer loss
of limb, of parent, of perfect child, of house,
of hope tethered to distant dreams.

Broken houses, churches, schools—
the splintered wood of people's lives
at odd angles gives odd consolation.
The community of grief is universal.

9/2/05

From *Inanna, Queen of Heaven and Earth*

*...the ways of the underworld are perfect.*
*They may not be questioned.*
        Neti, chief gatekeeper of the Kur

I am stitching together my dismembered self

with poems about you, my dismembered cat.

Like Inanna naked in the underworld,
hacked by her sister Ereshkigal
and hung on a meat hook
I've hung in the dark

my royal identity lost
treachery unfolding on all sides.
Alone, I've forgotten my name.

A gentle zephyr recalls you.
Your soft memory restores my breath.
If I can breathe, I can call the poem to life

and cling to its flying feet
as we rise in words—you and I—
from the hook of hell.

9/6/05

Do I dare visit your grave today to deliver asters and
    goldenrod
and read this poem, hoping you know how much we
    love you
and do not forget? How we walk the woods without you

listening for sounds, watching for changes of color and
    movement—
shifting leaves, a track, some scat—the woods no longer the
same without you. We were safe together, or so we foolish
    thought

before what came to be a wooden world
filled with shadowy shapes that could be glacial erratic,
animal body poised in camouflage stillness waiting to strike.

Then, we walked in a fragrant garden.
The snake has whispered, Death, and we are afraid.

When winter fills in forest spaces between trees
whose leaves are crushed under weight of snow,
we'll see clearly to reclaim the ground from what

took you away. We'll walk the trails and remember
your tail, hooked with joy as you followed and led
the way into what is now.

9/6/05

A lone phoebe clings to a branch
taking in the morning sun, when suddenly
human talk, its tones rising and falling
in words of walkers, breaks the Quaker silence

in a splash down from the ash's leaves
under the push of the lifting bird
into sunlight caught in the spotted
and yellow-turning leaves this morning

after the hurricane. Clouds are blown
to blue sky, no longer hidden
from human eye, rinsed clear by rain
and willing to see again what might be possible.

## Resurrection

*Early in the morning*
*on the first day of the week*
*while it was still dark ... John 21:1*

You describe the state of the Model A
pushed over and down the river bank
to become part of a family's history.

Brought to its resting place by one
of the brothers who knew
of your interest and restorer's soul,

he said he'd be glad of it taken away.
You're making your plans involving
a skidder to pull it up and onto

the flat, where you'll bring a trailer
to haul it away, as you've hauled
a lifetime of ruination for restoration

in studio, in shop; it's underway
in your mind. It's underway.

## Is This Adoption Legal?

Dr. Frankenstein you name yourself
as you piece together a 1930 Ford.

Like a patchwork quilt, piece by piece
from bumper to bumper you build.

Books with photos and diagrams
lie open around the house for reference

with stacks of magazines always at hand
for the images of crankcase and fender

you need; for the names and addresses
of dealers of car parts. When you spoke

to a friend long-distance, you mentioned
you'd adopted a car. That said it all.

Photograph of My Son in Brooklyn, 1995

O beautiful boy in the photo, Twin Towers looming
behind you across the East River, crowded with boats,
vehicles pressing their way over Brooklyn Bridge busy, busy,
while the viewer's eye can't help looking up with awful
knowledge of what will happen six years hence, when what
was beautiful once comes crumbling down, and there's no
hope of reconstruction of those tumbled towers with their
personal cargo burned and crushed to a lethal powder that
stings the lungs of workers, who in their hurry to save whom
they can among the broken, inhale the death of countless
others desiccated, seeking to be borne away from calamity,
from catastrophe, from the end of life as they'd known it.

And you, my son, what of you embodying life
on the other side of the river, seated innocent
above the fray, a trick of the camera having you
eye those distant towers as if you were Gulliver,
and they a Lilliputian pair affixed to your right
shoulder. It's all illusion except for the deaths
to come and the look of the young man you were
seated on a parapet above the river, eyeing
the future and what you thought it could be.

**September 11, 2018**


On this day of destruction, the Word comes down
as bodies came down through the sacred air
as the towers themselves came down in fire and dust

choking those running away in donated sneakers
those running barefoot to Brooklyn, to Bedford Stuy
running, running away to the future, to this anniversary

when we remember the runners, the jumpers
the hostages on the planes; the lovers of fire
who commandeered those planes, those misguided

ones who worshiped death. But a new altar arises
today, when the Word comes down as life, new life
these 17 years gone; new life in the womb

of the present moment. New life that is breath
for those in New York and beyond.

## Homing Pigeon

I thought I heard a child upstairs.
No, it must be the bird I heard,
the brown and white homing pigeon
you bought at the Common Ground Fair.

I hear it again, wings beating
against its makeshift cage, fashioned
to thwart its flight. Water dish flipped,
grain scattered, a wet mess to greet you
when you come home.

You at 17 wanting your freedom, throwing clothes
and loud music around your room like grain
and water. How soon, little bird, will you fly away?
And will you return like the homing pigeon
to this place where you early learned to fly?

# A Question

A wood swallow circled your head
today, twice, before it flew away,
returning to circle once again.
You ask, *What could it mean?*

Every evening, as myth is told,
transformed to swallow the goddess Isis
would circle the column in which
her husband and brother Osiris was bound.

Do you yourself as upright column
stand transfixed through days of glory
while flying around you the Bird of Paradise
wrings you with worried wing?

**Left with questions about ...**

stewardship of the land we bought
when we were barely old enough
to grasp the meaning of being stewards
of what we had been given.

With age comes understanding.
With age comes sense of responsibility
to history held in the rings of the oak
in the whorls of pine crowned with cones

and even deeper in glacial stones
raked across this land in a distant time,
all of it passing through our hands
like water, as do the passing years ...

And what we choose, our actions now
are the future for stewards who follow.

**Night Visitors**

It's the first week of February.
Wild apples picked in October
have shriveled into themselves.

No longer suitable for apple pie
we dump them out for the herd of deer
that haunted our woods through

January, scavenging among spruce,
standing on hind legs in the snow
to reach the buds of high-bush and tree.

There's no distinction on the ground—
everything was eaten as we found
the morning after a moonlit meal in Maine.

## After the Blizzard

Big boys muscle across the sky
in gangs of snow-laden clouds
losing their stormy power. What

have we left? Maybe an hour
of seeing these clouds released
back into the blue

becoming a memory of the storm
they were, dissipated, like old men
remembering how once
they rode the sky on horses.

## March, You've Arrived

dragging behind you a weather map's worth
of green and purple bands of snow and sleet,
of fog and rain confounding pundits of all things

weather. A drop in temperature and barometer
succeeded by a yard full of robins in snow,
your energy the antidote we need for cabin fever.

We welcome your challenge to change,
to turn in place and face another direction.

# The Battle for Spring

What dreams does he dream, this porcupine
asleep in the woodshed of my writing house
on this rainy morning in early March?

Does he dream of the first green shoots
of spring he dined on only last week
before cold descended again like the fist

of Odin, freezing streams and ponds
in a single night, and reclaiming seasonal
sovereignty, until this rain broke through
like a Viking horde?

**Gotcha!**

The north wind turns its pockets
inside out and rain becomes snow,
blown with hurricane force, flung
hurly-burly against the pane
and unwinding over the fields
in a full-throated howl. I hear
the chuckle of March, like Lucy
with her football. She's fooled
Charlie Brown once again.

## March 12

All is a-melt, including my soul
bound tight these months
by cords of cold that release it
gently, so as not to shock
with the feverish heat of change.

# Thoughts during a Snow Squall

The last of March blows wildly in
from the North, freezing us with a cold
and cleansing breath. Not ready to concede
the season to skipping lambs, it faces head
on the full-grown Aries.

Tired of painful cold, I yet covet the pure
company of this sudden snow. Not a little
in love with death, the prospect of blooming
life can overwhelm. An unnamed woman
slipped under the river's ice last week

after setting down her cellphone.
Life can become too much of a good thing.
She has entered the river—as will we all—
a prophetic action beyond recall.

## ShhShhhShhhh!

With a sudden rush of slush
    off the roof
the mind comes fully awake
and the body alive with surprise.

The temperature at 35
and the coming storm delayed
made room for nature to shovel

yesterday's snow. As with a good
sneeze, the system is shaken
as I am shaking now.

# Presque Isle, Maine: Snow, 5/16/16

The violets are blooming.
I thought I'd let you know.
Their purple heads are peeking
Above a late spring snow.

Brave citizens of a country
Where beauty is conceived,
They don't complain or whine
That spring is absent without leave.

**I Ask and Receive**

A phoebe rides the summer wind
on an outhanging branch of pine

while a fledgling phoebe appears
on the sill, its eye a bead beautiful

its feathered head like my grandson's
head, freshly out of bed and all uncombed.

## Birds in Wind

A knot, a snarl, a twist of birds
like so many words alight on my eye
describing themselves in joyful eruptions
of wings flung back on the wind.

## Tribulation

*It will go badly for pregnant and nursing women in those days.*
                                           *Mark 13: 17*
From a nest under the woodpile, a mouse runs out
when I move a stick. There goes another, scurrying
away, this one a mother with terrified eyes
her tiny baby still clinging to one of her teats
and towed like a water-skier behind a boat.
Freed from the tarp with its hiding places
mother and baby are lost in a sea of grass.

# Dalliance

24 inches head to tail, the snake
camouflaged in leafy detritus was couched
in the shadow of a looming hemlock.

Eye met eye and I was held for
moments by what seemed intelligence,
frightening in its mythic associations
circling my head like deerflies in July.

I broke off focus and walked away.
I'd been stared down but didn't mind
refocused as I was on the road ahead.

## O Holy Day!

*What then I saw is more than tongue can say.*
*Our human speech is dark before the vision.*
	*The Divine Comedy,* Dante Alighieri

As words failed Dante to describe Paradise
words fail me as I look to the woods
except for the barest verbal skeleton—
trees, brush, sunlight, shadow.

How common. How plain. How failed
a poet, who can only say thank you
for this holy day in mid-September
rife with aster and goldenrod
before the killing frost.

## Notice for Penobscot Bay, Maine

The ferry to Vinalhaven is cancelled
today. At a distance I wonder who or
what in the natural world is responsible
for the delay—the gale that has blown
for three days, lifting towers of gray
waves? Sickness? Death?
All old friends
to island dwellers who roll the dice
each day of life on this rocky ledge,
and on this green sea, where they
and fish meet to tell their stories.

## Thoughts in Late September

We all know the snow is coming
forthwith, when we will hunker down
in cave, in house, in cold cellar.

Like dried hydrangeas and goldenrod,
all in our rooms, we'll await the spring,
when re-seeded with life, we'll emerge
into the fervent light.

# A Child's Prayer

*If you don't destroy the world,*
*I will give you my life.*

Pricked with the point of a safety pin
my index finger dripping blood,
at nine years old I signed that note

I wrote and buried in a woodsy glade
where it rotted into the earth
with root and maggot.

Now at the other end of life
I look out onto a May-green field
bordered by ash and burgeoning lilac.

*The world blooms.*

You've kept your side of the bargain.
I've kept mine too, amazed to find
that giving over a life is life, not self-denial
fulfillment of a kind all unexpected.

## I Skirt the Violets

I skirt the violets
careful not to crush their delicate faces.
In so doing,
I step on dandelions,
an imposition of caste under my foot.

## May I Have This Dance?

Refuse the path of least resistance
and try another way, that of a child
learning to dance, balanced on the toes
of her father's Florsheims. What it is
about the dancing father that gives
the lie to Sternest Judge is the quiet
joy on the face of the daughter, who
trusts his sure step around the floor.

## Yes, Virginia, There Is a God

When I was a child, I wished for a house
a small house in the woods where I could write.

I made the wish on no star, prayed to no god per se;
it was simply the unspoken wish of a child's heart

brought to mind on a latter day
when I was grown and walking home

from my writing house on the edge of the woods.
Understanding came in a moment complete:
I had the desire of my heart.

# Deep into April

Easter is three weeks old,
old enough to stand on its legs
and walk the landscape speaking life
into dead grasses, reluctant buds and
icy hearts of men who have given up.

Easter is what it does:
renews to left, right, and center.
Its seamless garment passing over,
the grass goes green.

**Housekeeping**

Someone is in the house. Uninvited.
Not feeling threatened, but uncomfortable
and needing to know who it is because
a young child, full of trust, as children are
is busy in all the rooms of the house
and could easily be discovered
by someone else.

*You! What are you doing here?*
*Why didn't you leave when the party was over?*
*This is not your home.*

Your quick smile, your red shirt, your evasive
eyes, your glossy attempts to explain
your presence. Your resistance to leaving—
more than that—your insistence on staying
is as clear as your dancing feet that tap
into room after room as I follow you,
with a broom meant for cleaning.

## Lost in Limbo

Outside these cemetery gates
guarded by angels of stone, unbaptized
infants were once buried, unable
to be interred in hallowed ground
because of original sin not washed away.

Not knowing how to be merciful
and just, rule makers wrote them
into the margin of books that held
the question open—in limbo,
Latin for margin—which hardened
to doctrine of a secondary heaven
where needs were met for these innocent
babes, who because no one thought
to baptize— even with spittle,
in an emergency, as Sister said—
would be separated from God forever.

Lord, have mercy on all of us
who subscribed to such a belief about you
who from the first and to the last
is source of comfort for grieving parents
then and now, when the height, length, and
depth of your love is medicament
for this most grievous wound, as you dig
with your hands in the earth you created

to hollow out a hole the size of love
to receive the body; then do you gather up
the perfect soul and return with it to home.

# A Dream After My Mother's Death

I was afraid at first of the young hart
coming at me with head down

in what looked like an attitude of attack.
The woods behind him, the field behind me

I could have turned and run
but I stood my ground.

He pawed his ground. I ran to the side
and he, seeing my move, came after me

and I, seeing his, now ran, noticing
for the first time that it was night.

While a million stars distracted me
he butted me gently with his small

horns, and I sensed us lifting off the ground.
We were flying. I let fall my drawn-up legs

loosened my grip on his soft neck
and held it in a friendly way

and like him, looking straight ahead
took in the night, loved the night,

was one with the night, and seeing
somehow those below moving

in the field we flew above. I wanted
to tell my mother and searched the faces

for sight of hers, and there she was
looking up and smiling.

## You Can Get There from Here

I return to the cellar nightly
pressing my cupped ear
against the unyielding side
of the water heater.

I crouch in the dark.
Gurgle and hum inside the tank
summon words sleeping within me
in waters older than time.

Mothers collectively cross my mind.
I rise, I walk,
I follow them through the dark
sensing my way.

## To Eat or Be Eaten

Black-flies enter my writing house.
Too numerous to count, they hurry
across and up and down the window panes
fitfully seeking escape, unaware of the spider
two panes over, watching to see how well
its webbing will work.
The black-flies flew
through the open door. Granted they didn't
know of the spider, but fly they did, and walk
they will into the webbing. The room throbs
with inevitability. They will be etherized
like Eliot's patient upon the table, as will we
for better or worse in the end.

# Tightrope Walking

In Pearl Buck's *The Good Earth,*
the protagonist and his wife have had a child,
a much desired son. They walk along
talking excitedly about their beautiful boy.

Suddenly, fearfully they realize what
they are doing. The mother tucks
the baby out of sight, and together
she and her husband lament

the misshapen, unfortunate child,
hoping to deflect the gods'
vengeance and not to tempt foul fate.

A partridge setting on a nest
with chicks warm beneath her wing.
would understand. With danger near
she would cry out and feign wounded

wing, 'round and around she'd run
to distract a predator from discovering
and destroying her chicks.

My mother too a fatalist, a strategist
and dealmaker with the gods, when
approaching a stop light that shone green
would begin her litany of denial: It'll never last.

It'll be red by the time we get there.
You'll see. Eureka. The light still green
on our arrival, she'd drive on through
the intersection shaking her head

with a small victory chuckle. Either way
she won. She'd be right or she'd be happy
to take what the gods had offered that day,
more than enough for her.

# Parallels

I saw on TV a scientist
enclosed by choice with a male gorilla
the only breeder in captivity
who tolerates human beings.

The two rolled in the hay and wrestled
the gorilla master of the play,
the scientist pointing out in passing
the gorilla was using just two percent

of his strength and five percent of his
biting power. The scientist confided
during the hour that when he takes
his bath at night, there are chains

of bruises up and down his arms.
When Jacob wrestling the angel
was permanently wounded in the hip,
how much strength did the angel

not use and why did he choose not
to use it? And how much is Yahweh
holding back? How much love remains
hidden, lest by uncovering his face

he ravish his beloved to the point of death?
I remember the night in dream, when I chose
death if it meant life, lunging out, impaling myself
on the finial at the foot of the bed, unaware

of pain 'til the next day when creeping bruise
mottled my left side. Like Jacob rubbing
his arthritic hip later in life, I treasure the knot
of bone that marks the place of the break
        that's mended now.

## In the Woods

*A Japanese study revealed forest landscapes
are therapeutic and reduce stress.*

Steady yourself with trees.
Grasp the lower branches and hold on.
Yes, like that. Greet the hemlock
without fear. (Think Socrates.)

You can pass through a woods
entire this way, going from tree
to tree over rough ground,
your moving-forward steps

inevitable in a life lived beyond
the steps of what you've called
your home, and on to the home
on the other side of this great
woods you have already entered.

(Don't even think about turning back.)
Even now the sun is gone; darkness
settles like an old friend into your
common soul. Steady yourself
now with the presence of trees.

## For a Friend: R.I.P.

It's nearly five years since you left
heralded by the promise of sun
still beneath the December horizon
but soon to rise in full radiance

lighting the path of your journey out.
Wherever that "out" is, you are there.
The drama of grieving done, I
approach that same threshold

without fear, only trust, and mini-
mum curiosity, knowing I must work
while I have the light. Soon enough night
will come, and then no work will be

done. Is that how it is for you: Done?
Or are the stories of busy saints true?
Is the absence of clocked time a boon
that allows you to do what you will

for "hours" on end? Come back to the
desk, I tell myself. Pick up the pen
and work on the poems. Honor her
and her work by doing your own.

# Father's Day

At 6 o'clock in the morning the phone rings.
He has not been asleep or dreaming, but is
nevertheless in a somewhat hypnotic state.

In his mind's eye he sees the man
swimming hard across the channel,
body resisting the pull of the tide.

Arm over arm, feet a-paddle, driving
driving across the water. He watches
and wonders at what he sees.

The swimmer reaches the far bank,
climbs out of the water to stand up-
right, and turns, his arms in the air

victorious. I made it, he says aloud.
The man, his father, knows his son
and answers the phone, only to find him gone.

## And Then?

Just that quick—snap!—dissolution.
A post-it note into the fire.
Crackle. Snap. Gone. Done.
Over. It's over, and so are you.

No more wakings and sleepings
now. The die is cast. It's over.
Cleanse yourself while you live
and remember to forgive yourself

as well as others. What happens
then is not your concern. A post-it
note consigned is what I'm saying.

## Hello, Goodbye

Off you go on your tractor to split the wood.
Seems I'm always hailing you from a distance,
you at your work, I at mine watching you,
recording your work on a day in spring
that is already looking through summer
to the cold trap of winter beyond, knowing
the flare of color in fall a brief fire
that will not last but will end as we will—
brown and sere—pushed off our branch
by the buds of another spring.

## To Bury or Burn

To bury or burn drafts of poems
stacked two feet high in my writing house—
I have no illusion of them being sought
by academy, library, or even family.

So what's the point of saving them
and not throwing them in the recycling
bin, onto the town dump, or into the stove?
How quickly those piles of poems
would burn to ash.

I choose not to burn but to bury,
honoring the work by giving its shaping
back to the earth from which it sprang—
a witness to the promise of resurrection.

## Author's Note

Judith Robbins continues to write in the writing house pictured on the cover of this, her newest collection of poems. Her husband built this "room of one's own" for her over 40 years ago when they first moved to Whitefield. A young couple raising their four children at that time, she was able to pay the money needed for the construction by cashing in a life insurance policy her mother had bought for her when she was a child. It wasn't enough money to change the world, but it was enough to change her small corner of it.

What does one do with years of drafts of poems written in that house? With boxes and bags of letters and mementos from a long life of relationships? This book answers that question.

www.ingramcontent.com/pod-product-compliance
Lightning Source LLC
LaVergne TN
LVHW041343080426
835512LV00006B/599